||| || ||||| ||||||||||||||||||||||||||||||
W9-AZC-882

STECK-VAUGHN
PORTRAIT OF AMERICA

Pacific Islands

973
POR

Pacific Islands C 3

~~Schuyler Library and Media Center~~
~~The Doane Stuart School~~
~~99 Academy Road~~
Albany, NY 12208

Copyright © 1996 Steck-Vaughn Company

All rights reserved. No part of this book may be reproduced or utilized in any form or by any means, electronic or mechanical, including photocopying, recording, or by any information storage and retrieval system, without permission in writing from the copyright owner. Requests for permission to make copies of any part of the work should be mailed to: Copyright Permissions, Steck-Vaughn Company, P.O. Box 26015, Austin, Texas 78755.

Steck-Vaughn Company

Executive Editor	Diane Sharpe
Senior Editor	Martin S. Saiewitz
Design Manager	Pamela Heaney
Photo Editor	Margie Foster
Electronic Cover Graphics	Alan Klemp

Proof Positive/Farrowlyne Associates, Inc.
Program Editorial, Revision Development, Design, and Production

Consultants: Nikolao Pula, Debbie Suber-Wiggins, Joseph McDermott, Frank Quimby, United States Department of the Interior, Office of Insular Affairs

Published by Raintree Steck-Vaughn Publishers, an imprint of Steck-Vaughn Company.

A Turner Educational Services, Inc. book. Based on the Portrait of America television series by R. E. (Ted) Turner.

Cover Photo: Two Lover's Point by © Superstock.

Cartography: Pacific Islands Map by Maryland Cartographics.

Library of Congress Cataloging-in-Publication Data

Thompson, Kathleen.
    Pacific Islands / Katherine Kristen.
      p. cm. — (Portrait of America)
    "Based on the Portrait of America television series" — T.p. verso.
    "A Turner book."
    Includes index.
    ISBN 0-8114-7398-8 (library binding). — ISBN 0-8114-7479-8 (softcover)
      1. Guam—Juvenile literature. 2. Northern Mariana Islands—
Juvenile literature. 3. American Samoa—Juvenile literature.
[1. Guam. 2. Northern Mariana Islands. 3. American Samoa.
4. Oceania.] I. Portrait of America (Television program)
II. Title. III. Series: Thompson, Kathleen. Portrait of America.
DU17.T48 1996
966.7—dc20

           95-26299
           CIP
           AC

Printed and Bound in the United States of America

1 2 3 4 5 6 7 8 9 10 WZ 98 97 96 95

Acknowledgments
The publishers wish to thank the following for permission to reproduce photographs:
Pp. 7, 8 © Superstock; p. 10 (top) The Bettmann Archive, (bottom) The Bishop Museum; pp. 11, 12 © Superstock; p. 13 (top) © Steve Vidler/Leo de Wys, (bottom) The Bishop Museum; pp. 14, 15 (both) UPI/Bettmann; p. 16 (top) UPI/Bettmann, (bottom) © Superstock; p. 17 © Steve Vidler/Leo de Wys; p. 18 National Portrait Gallery, Smithsonian Institution; p. 19 © James Sugar/Black Star; p. 21 © Superstock; p. 22 (both) The Bishop Museum; p. 23 © Don Smetzer/Tony Stone Images; p. 24 © Superstock; p. 26 © Byron Crader/Ric Ergenbright Photography; p. 27 The Bishop Museum; p. 28 (top) © Superstock, (bottom) © Steve Vidler/Leo de Wys; p. 29 © Glen Allison/Tony Stone Images; p. 31 (top) © Byron Crader/Ric Ergenbright Photography, (bottom) © Al Grotell; pp. 32, 33 © Al Grotell; p. 34 © Superstock; p. 36 (top) © David Hiser/Tony Stone Images, (bottom) © Steve Vidler/Leo de Wys; p. 37 (top) © Keith Ogata, (bottom) © David Austen/Tony Stone Images; p. 38 © Superstock; p. 39 © David Austen/Tony Stone Images; pp. 40, 41 © Don Smetzer/Tony Stone Images; p. 42 © Byron Crader/Ric Ergenbright Photography; p. 44 © Superstock; p. 46 (both) One Mile Up.

STECK-VAUGHN
PORTRAIT OF AMERICA

Pacific Islands

Katherine Kristen

A Turner Book

RSVP
RAINTREE
STECK-VAUGHN
PUBLISHERS
The Steck-Vaughn Company

Austin, Texas

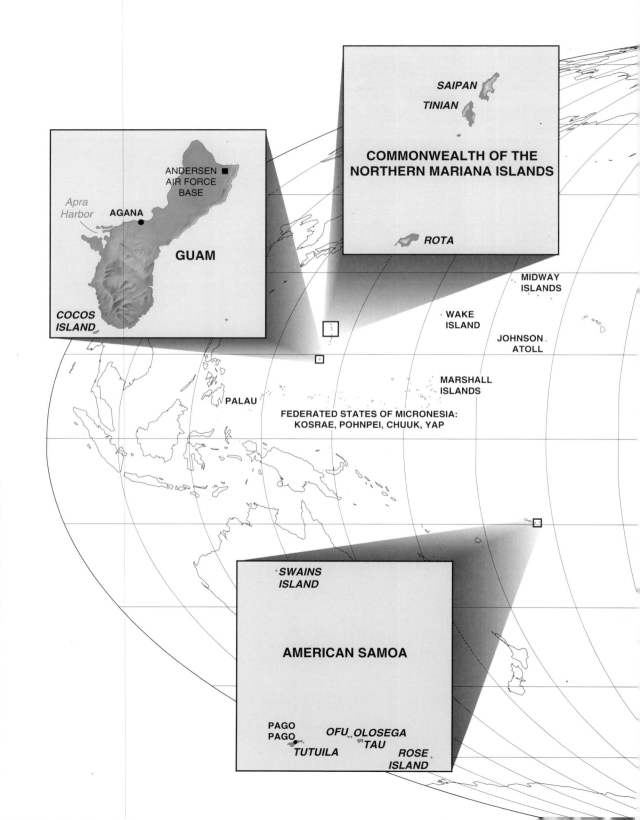

Pacific Islands

ANDERSEN
AIR FORCE
BASE

Apra
Harbor

AGANA

GUAM

COCOS
ISLAND

SAIPAN
TINIAN

COMMONWEALTH OF THE
NORTHERN MARIANA ISLANDS

ROTA

MIDWAY
ISLANDS

WAKE
ISLAND

JOHNSON
ATOLL

PALAU

MARSHALL
ISLANDS

FEDERATED STATES OF MICRONESIA:
KOSRAE, POHNPEI, CHUUK, YAP

SWAINS
ISLAND

AMERICAN SAMOA

PAGO
PAGO

OFU OLOSEGA
TAU

TUTUILA

ROSE
ISLAND

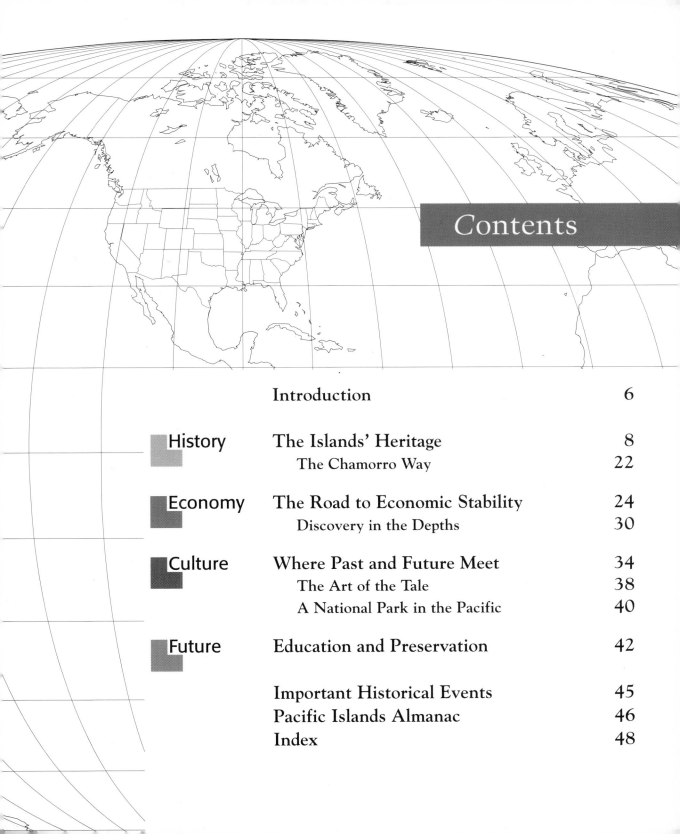

Contents

Introduction

The Pacific Ocean is dotted with hundreds of islands spread across millions of square miles of ocean. The United States has special relationships with some of these islands including Guam, the Commonwealth of the Northern Marianas, and American Samoa. Since the end of World War II, the United States has also been associated with the island nations of Palau, the Marshall Islands, and the Federated States of Micronesia.

The Pacific Islands are a blend of tradition, progress, and natural beauty. Rain forests and miles of white beaches mingle with modern business centers and early Spanish architecture. The Pacific Islanders are proud of their association with the United States. In Guam they say *Hafa Adai*, a greeting that welcomes everyone to a culture of tradition and modern living.

In 1669 Guam's Plaza de España was the Spanish governor's palace. Later, in 1941, it was the place where American armed forces surrendered to Japanese troops.

Pacific Islands

The Islands' Heritage

About 3,500 years ago, China, seeking to expand its empire, began a mass migration into Southeast Asia. Many Asian people did not want to be ruled by the Chinese, however. Some people built canoes with sails and set out into the Pacific Ocean, hoping to find a new home. They were in search of a place like the one they were used to, with clean water, good soil, and plenty of fish. They found what they were looking for on a group of islands many miles away in the Pacific. Today these islands are known as Guam and the Northern Marianas. There the people settled, living mainly on fish at first, and later developing agriculture.

The first inhabitants of this group of islands were called *Chamorros* by the Spanish. Archaeological artifacts found on the footprint-shaped island of Guam are the oldest in the Western Pacific. They include pieces of limestone pillars that scientists believe served as supports for houses belonging to the wealthy. Most Chamorros lived in small villages ruled by local chiefs.

These are latte stones, prehistoric coral pillars that held up the houses of wealthy Chamorros as long ago as A.D. 500.

Ferdinand Magellan's journey across the Pacific Ocean took much longer than he expected. By the time Magellan and his crew reached the Pacific Islands, they were sick from scurvy.

The earliest written history of present-day Guam dates back to 1521. In that year, Ferdinand Magellan of Spain stopped at the island while making the world's very first sailing voyage around the globe. He anchored only briefly at Umatac Bay on the island's southwestern shore. He named the island and all the surrounding islands *Ladrones*, which means "thieves," because he claimed the people there stole a small boat from him. Forty-four years later, in 1565, another Spaniard, Miguel López de Legazpi, arrived and claimed these islands for Spain. He renamed them the *Marianas* in honor of Mariana of Austria, who was then regent, or temporary ruler, of Spain.

Spanish colonization did not begin right away; the people of the islands were left in peace for another one hundred years. In 1668 Spanish Jesuit missionaries began to arrive. They tried to introduce Christianity to the Chamorros. Converting the Chamorros proved a difficult task, so the Spanish used force. From 1680 to 1695, Spanish troops in the command of José de Quinoga waged war on the islanders. The Spanish

This engraving shows Christians outside an early Jesuit mission in Guam. The first Catholic mass held in Guam took place more than 450 years ago.

The beautiful countryside on American Samoa can be seen from the cliffs overlooking Pago Pago Harbor.

troops outnumbered the Chamorros and fought with guns, while the Chamorros used only their handmade weapons. In addition, the Chamorros were weakened by the European diseases brought to the islands by the Spanish over the years. The combination of these deadly factors was too much for the Chamorros. Between 1668 and 1741, their population dropped from eighty thousand to less than five thousand. Present-day Guam and the Mariana Islands remained Spanish colonies until 1898.

The group of volcanic islands known collectively as the Samoan Islands lies to the southeast of Guam and the Marianas. A Dutch admiral named Jacob Roggeveen discovered the Samoan Islands in 1722. He miscalculated the islands' location, however, and Samoa stayed isolated for another 46 years. In 1768 French navigator Louis-Antoine de Bougainville charted the exact position of the islands. Soon ships from many countries began arriving in Samoa.

In 1839 a United States naval commander named Charles Wilkes brought a scientific expedition to

Samoa. He made maps of the islands and recorded plants and wildlife. Wilkes also helped the Samoan chiefs create a list of rules to guide the behavior of visiting ships. One chief, Malietoa Vainu'upo, expressed his gratitude to Wilkes by allowing him to raise the United States flag in the harbor city of Pago Pago. But this was only a friendly gesture; the Samoans also welcomed British and German ships. In fact, so many ships stopped in Samoa that it soon became clear that whichever nation controlled trading rights stood to gain huge profits. This caused a lot of tension between the trio of nations most interested in those rights.

In 1879 a group of Samoan chiefs granted Germany almost complete control of the harbor near Apia. Later that year, another group of chiefs gave Great Britain the right to build a naval station in the same area. The chiefs fought among themselves, and the three nations continued the debate over control of the islands. By 1889 tensions were so high that the United States, Great Britain, and Germany each had warships anchored not far off the coast. Samoa's history might have been very different if a hurricane had not devastated the area that year. It hit the islands full force and sunk many United States and German ships. Many people on the islands were killed. This event actually helped to bring about a spirit of peace among the feuding nations. Instead of going to war, they

Pago Pago has one of the best deep-water harbors in the South Pacific. The surrounding mountains protect the harbor from damaging winds, and its bowl shape shelters it from high waves.

decided to resolve their differences at a conference held in Berlin. On June 14, 1889, the Berlin treaty made the Samoan Islands a neutral territory, to be ruled by a Samoan king. Foreign countries would control only the areas they had already bought from the Samoans.

The arrangement didn't last long. Despite the king, individual chiefs continued to hold power in Samoa. The chiefs could not agree on land rights, and war broke out among them. In 1899 the Berlin treaty was overturned. A new agreement was signed on December 2, 1899. It gave eastern Samoa to the United States and western Samoa to Germany. Between 1900 and 1904, the chiefs of eastern Samoa signed over their authority to the United States. The area was renamed American Samoa.

For many years, the Pacific Islands' location kept them isolated from technology—and from news of the world. In June 1898, during the Spanish-American War, Captain Henry Glass sailed into Guam's Apra Harbor with orders to capture the island. Guam was still a Spanish colony at this time. The Guamanians had not known that Spain and the United States were at war. The governor of Guam surrendered immediately. Less than a month later, on August 12, 1898, the Treaty

During the nineteenth century, Spanish troops used this stone sentry box, overlooking Guam's Umatac Bay, to scan the ocean for invaders.

This engraving shows Guam in the days of early European contact, with a fort on the bluff, a European sailboat in the foreground, and traditional Pacific Island canoes to the left.

13

of Paris was signed. This treaty made Guam a possession of the United States. By this time Guam was politically separate from the Mariana Islands, which Spain had sold to Germany in 1899.

From 1898 to 1941, Guam served as a United States naval station. It was run by a series of federally appointed governors. These governors answered to the United States President, not to the Guamanian people. Then in 1930, a democratic-minded governor wrote up a bill of rights for Guam. The document was approved in 1933. Although not all the later governors followed the bill of rights closely, it did allow the island's people some say in their own government.

The Northern Marianas were controlled by various countries over the course of history. After Germany's World War I defeat in 1918, the Treaty of Versailles gave control of the Northern Marianas to Japan. The Japanese fortified the islands and eventually used them as the launch site for the 1941 bombing of Pearl Harbor

Flames and smoke surround the U.S.S. *West Virginia* and the U.S.S. *Tennessee* after Japan attacked Pearl Harbor on December 7, 1941. The United States declared war on Japan the next day.

in Hawaii. This bombing brought the United States into World War II.

Wake Island and its sister islands, Wilkes and Peale, had been claimed by the United States in 1898. The islands were used as a telegraph station on the route between San Francisco, California, and Manila, in the Philippines. In 1935 the islands served as an air base for planes crossing the Pacific Ocean. When the United States entered World War II, the islands became a military target. On the same day that Japanese forces bombed Pearl Harbor, they also bombed Wake Island. Four hundred United States Marines and about a thousand civilians resisted a Japanese invasion for two weeks. But the Japanese were finally able to capture Wake Island. They remained there until 1945 when Japan surrendered, ending the war.

Despite its strategic location, Guam was not well defended at the beginning of World War II. Japanese forces bombed Guam on the same day they bombed Pearl Harbor and Wake Island, December 7, 1941. Ten thousand Japanese troops landed on Guam after the bombing. Three days later American troops surrendered. American soldiers took back the island on August 10, 1944, after three weeks of fighting. Not all Japanese soldiers surrendered so easily, however. Some remained inside the Guamanian jungle for years. One diehard sergeant named Shoichi Yokoi hid out in the jungle until 1972. He didn't realize until then that the war had ended.

above. The United States 77th Army Division marches through the jungle on Guam's Liberation Day during World War II. More than 2,000 Americans, 18,000 Japanese, and 150 Guamanians died in the liberation.

below. Japanese army sergeant Shoichi Yokoi hid in a cave in Guam's jungle for 28 years.

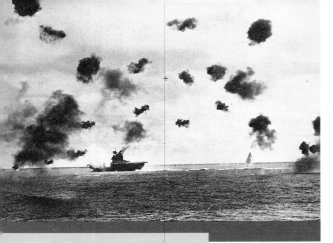

The United States knew Japan was planning an attack on Midway Island because it cracked the secret code used by Japan's navy. When Japanese forces arrived, the United States Navy was waiting to ambush them.

This peace memorial on Saipan was erected in honor of the five million people who died fighting in the Pacific during World War II.

With the removal of the Japanese, Guam became the headquarters of the Pacific Naval Forces, which were commanded by Admiral Chester W. Nimitz. By 1945 there were more than two hundred thousand military personnel living on Guam.

During World War II, twenty thousand American troops were posted on American Samoa to guard against a Japanese invasion. The invasion never happened, but United States soldiers stayed until the war was over. Living side by side with American culture brought many changes to the village traditions of the Samoan people. Many Samoans went to work for the military. They combined American food, clothing, and technology with their own culture.

The United States maintained many military bases in the Pacific. One of the most important was Midway. This area is made up of two small islands, Eastern and Sand. The United States discovered the islands in 1859 and obtained them in 1867. On June 6, 1942, United States forces led by Admiral Nimitz defeated Japanese forces near Midway. Four Japanese aircraft carriers were sunk during the battle. Only one United States carrier—the *Yorktown*—was downed. The Battle of Midway marked the first major United States victory against Japan in World War II.

The Northern Marianas islands of Saipan and Tinian became important take-off points for United States bombing missions during World War II. On August 6, 1945, an American B-29 bomber, the *Enola Gay*, took off from the island of Tinian. Hours later it dropped an atomic bomb on the Japanese city of Hiroshima. On August 9, United States forces dropped a second atomic bomb—this time on the Japanese port city of Nagasaki. The bombings brought an end to World War II. Today, one of the most famous World War II monuments in the Pacific stands on the island of Tinian.

This is the Agat Invasion Marker located within War in the Pacific National Park in Guam. It marks one of the sites where liberating forces landed in 1944.

In 1947 the newly-formed United Nations grouped the Japanese-held Micronesian islands into a United States-run trust territory. This trust territory was to be governed by the United States until the time that each island district could freely choose another status. The trust territory consisted of several groups of islands including the Caroline Islands and Marshall Islands. In 1986 the Caroline Islands set up an independent government. According to the terms of the agreement between the islands and the United States, the Caroline Islands were divided into the Palau Islands and the Federated States of Micronesia (FSM). The FSM includes the islands of Yap, Kosrae, Chuuk, and Pohnpei. That same year the Marshall Islands and the United States came to a similar agreement, and these islands became known as the Republic of the Marshall Islands (RMI).

17

On December 22, 1990, the United Nations Security Council officially ended the trusteeship—for all of the districts except Palau. Palau's political status was argued until 1994. On October 1 of that year, Palau was made an independent nation. Weeks later its government applied to the United Nations requesting membership. The remaining districts of the former trust territory have agreed to Compacts of Free Association with the United States. This means that the islands are self-governed, but they also receive economic aid from the United States. In return for this aid, the United States maintains the right to build military bases and control defense in the area. It also has the responsibility of protecting the citizens of the freely associated territories against foreign military invasion.

The Northern Marianas were also a part of the United Nations trust territories. In 1975 citizens of the Northern Marianas voted for political union with the United States. A new constitution went into effect in 1978. Residents of the Marianas were then eligible for United States citizenship. On November 3, 1986, the United States and the Northern Marianas approved an agreement that establishes the Northern Marianas as a commonwealth. This measure officially ended the United Nations trusteeship of the Northern Marianas. As a commonwealth, the Northern Marianas govern their own internal affairs. But the United States controls the islands' foreign affairs, including defense. Only four of the fourteen islands of the Northern Marianas are inhabited. The largest and the most populated of this island group are Saipan, Tinian, and

In 1947 President Truman signed the Trusteeship Agreement for the Northern Marianas. The agreement provided for the islands to be under the control of the United States Navy.

18

The four volcanic islands of the Northern Marianas were formed by lava overflow. The others are made of coral.

Rota. Only about one hundred people out of the entire Northern Marianas population of about 45,000 live elsewhere. Four uninhabited islands belonging to this group—Pagan, Anatahan, Asuncion, and Farallon de Pajaros—are active volcanoes.

In 1950 President Harry S. Truman signed the Organic Act, which gave the territory of Guam a new form of government. The people of Guam were made United States citizens. Because of naval restrictions, however, no one was allowed to visit Guam without a military security pass. Planes were allowed to land and refuel, but passengers were not allowed to leave the airport. This limited the development of private industries, especially tourism. The restrictions were lifted in 1962, and soon after, an international airport was opened near Guam's capital, Agana. A wide variety of industries has since taken hold, including tourism, ship repairs, textile manufacturing, publishing, and printing. In 1970 Guamanians voted into office their first elected governor. Guam voted to seek United States commonwealth status in 1982. For now, it remains an unincorporated, organized United States territory. It is "unincorporated" because not all the provisions of the United States Constitution apply to the territory. It is "organized" because the Organic Act of 1950 organized the government in much the same way a constitution would. Guam has one elected, nonvoting delegate in the United States House of Representatives.

American Samoa is an unorganized and unincorporated territory of the United States. Located 2,300 miles south of Honolulu, Hawaii, it is the farthest south of all United States-owned territories. Congress never provided American Samoa with an Organic Act, which would have organized the American Samoan government along the lines of a constitution. In 1951 President Truman shifted responsibility for the islands from the United States Navy to the Department of the Interior. American Samoa developed quickly after that. Many schools and housing projects were built, and a vast system of paved roads was created. The people of American Samoa are considered United States nationals, not citizens. This means they may not vote in United States presidential elections. American Samoa elects one nonvoting representative to Congress. Today more than one third of American Samoa's working force are employed by the American Samoa government. Nearly one third more work for the booming tuna industries, and the remainder work for private businesses.

Other United States territories include Johnston Atoll and the Midway and Wake islands. Each of these

Agana, Guam's capital, has become a thriving tourist destination in the 1990s.

currently is run by a branch of the United States military. Johnston Atoll is an unorganized, unincorporated territory of the United States. It is governed by the Defense Nuclear Agency, a branch of the Nuclear Regulatory Commission. Wake Island, with a population of about 1,600, has been run by the United States Air Force since 1972. The Midway Islands are administered by the Department of the Navy. Most of the 2,200 residents of Midway and Wake islands are United States military personnel.

The American territories in the Pacific Islands played a dramatic part in the history of the United States. But they are much more than small pieces in a large puzzle. The islands have maintained many aspects of their original cultures, despite American influence. These unique people have found a way to keep the traditions of their ancestors alive, while accepting the modern approach to the twenty-first century.

The Chamorro Way

The earliest inhabitants of Guam were the Chamorros. About 3,500 years ago, these people left Southeast Asia and paddled across a vast stretch of the Pacific Ocean in wooden canoes. These vessels were probably stitched together with coconut-fiber rope and rigged with sails of woven leaves. How the Chamorros were able to navigate up to 1,200 miles in open sea without any instruments is a marvel of traditional navigation skills. They studied the stars to hold their direction and charted the pattern of water birds and ocean currents to plot their course. They found a land that was friendly to their way of life— a place with excellent fishing and a good climate for growing crops.

The Chamorros lived in villages grouped into districts. Each district was governed by a chief. There was a strong class system. The upper class was made up of chiefs and warriors. Fishermen, craftsmen, and other professionals made up the middle class. There was little contact between the classes. Marriage between classes was forbidden.

The Chamorros lived by a very strong code of what they considered proper behavior. The golden rule of their society was "It is better to ask for something and be refused than to be given something and refuse it." The people were careful and polite to one another. They made bonds of friendship that were nearly as strong as those of blood relations.

Some Chamorro groups made pottery out of basalt, which is a dark gray or black volcanic rock.

Not much is known about the ancient Chamorro religion. The people celebrated special days with food, prayer, dances, and games. They sang their myths and legends and held competitions based on who could remember the most verses.

When the Spanish missionaries arrived in Guam in 1668, they found a culture that was both intelligent and skillful. Over time, the missionaries converted the Chamorros to the Roman Catholic faith. Catholicism is still practiced in Guam.

Descendants of the ancient Chamorros make up a little less than half of Guam's present-day population. The strict class system no longer exists. Family remains a very important part of the modern Chamorro culture. However, the government now has many of the powers and responsibilities that were once associated with the family or the local chiefs. Social festivities still play a large part in Chamorro society. The people treat outsiders with great hospitality, often inviting complete strangers to attend their local festivities. Just as in ancient times, these gatherings serve to maintain the closeness between family, friends, and neighbors.

These American Samoans are celebrating Independence Day in Pago Pago. Like the Chamorros, American Samoans have maintained their traditional culture as much as possible since European contact.

The Road to Economic Stability

Guam's economy depends mainly on tourism and United States military spending. The island's geographic position—with Russian, Japanese, and Chinese borders located not far to the north—has made it strategically important. The United States maintains Andersen Air Force Base and several naval facilities on Guam. There are 21,000 United States military personnel and their families in residence there. Perhaps not surprisingly, Guam's monetary system is based on the American dollar.

Since the days of the Spanish-American War, Guam has been linked to the United States military. After World War II, the military created many jobs for the Guamanian people. Streets and a highway system were built to connect Andersen Air Force Base with other bases, such as the submarine base in Apra Harbor. At the same time, there was a push to build bigger and better schools. For example, the College of Guam opened its doors in 1952.

Blue lagoons and white sand beaches are why nearly one million tourists visit Guam every year. These people are relaxing at peaceful Tumon Beach.

Pacific Island airports, like Yap Airport in the western Caroline Islands, are important to island economies because most supplies and exports are shipped by air.

In early 1994 the United States military began to slowly cut back its operations in the Pacific Islands. This continues to present a threat to Guam's economic balance. For Guamanians, it will mean a transition from military jobs to tourism and other private businesses. Only about sixty percent of the Guamanian workforce is employed in the private sector, or nongovernment businesses. The other forty percent work for the Guamanian government or the federal government. As the United States military continues to scale back, those percentages are likely to change. The people of Guam are in the process of building up the private sector to offset the change in military spending. These private-sector industries include tourism, shipping services, printing and publishing, food processing, and textiles. Perhaps Guam's greatest hope of a stable economic future lies in its tourist industry. More tourists visit Guam than any of the other Pacific Islands, except Hawaii. The mild climate, fine beaches, and excellent surfing and scuba diving provide plenty of attractions.

Since the 1970s, tourism has expanded greatly, creating a boom in the construction of new hotels.

Visitors to Guam number more than one million a year. Because of Guam's nearness to Japan, eighty percent of these tourists are Japanese. Since the early 1990s, however, a slowdown in Japan's economic growth has been reflected in a slowdown in Guam's tourism. In August 1992, Guam's tourist image suffered when the island was hit by typhoon Omar. This tropical storm destroyed more than nine hundred homes and left two thousand families homeless. The damage to the island was estimated at between $113 million and $400 million. Although most of the island's hotels were reopened one month after the storm, the number of yearly visitors has declined.

After World War II, much of Guam's agricultural land was taken over to be used for military bases. Today, agriculture remains somewhat undeveloped. About 75 percent of Guam's food and industrial goods are imported from the United States.

In 1961 the United States government launched a program to develop the economy in American Samoa. At that time, many Samoans moved away from rural villages to seek jobs in the cities. Thatch-roof buildings were torn down and replaced by modern buildings better able to withstand the force of hurricanes. New schools were built. New roads were constructed, and old roads were repaired or paved.

In American Samoa, as in Guam, the economy is still strongly linked to the United States

This 1825 engraving depicts a distillery in Guam. Today, Guamanian manufacturers that produce alcoholic beverages must be licensed by Guam's Alcoholic Beverage Control Board.

Tourists relax at the pool area of the Rainmaker Hotel in Pago Pago, American Samoa. The Rainmaker Hotel is popular with tourists because it is near the aerial tram to American Samoa National Park.

government. American Samoa conducts eighty to ninety percent of its foreign trade with the United States and uses American currency. The backbone of American Samoa's industry is tuna fishing and fish processing. The territory's main export is canned tuna, which accounts for 93 percent of its export revenues.

Tourism didn't really begin in American Samoa until the 1960s, when a jet airport and the first luxury hotel were built there. Tourism is slowly becoming an economic force in the islands, however. So far though, American Samoa has not had the success that Guam and the Northern Marianas have had with tourism.

The Commonwealth of the Northern Marianas, like Guam and American Samoa, uses American currency and has historically received substantial financial

A tourist gazes at Umatac, Guam, from across the bay. Tourists in Umatac often cross the bay to see fortifications built by the Japanese during World War II.

assistance from the federal government. From 1986 to 1992 the United States and the Northern Marianas had an agreement that entitled the islands to $228 million in federal aid. These funds were used for development, government operations, and special programs.

Pago Pago is the only modern urban center on American Samoa.

The Northern Marianas' tourist industry has grown rapidly. About half the workforce in the Northern Marianas is currently employed within this thriving industry. As in Guam, the majority of tourists come from Japan. And, as in Guam, the long-term effects of Japan's economic slowdown on the islands' tourism remain to be seen.

Agriculture in the Northern Marianas consists mainly of cattle ranches and small farms. Important crops include coconuts, breadfruit, tomatoes, and melons. Saipan in particular has developed a strong textile and clothing manufacturing industry.

For the most part, the Pacific Islands have limited land available for creating a more varied economy. The gentle climate and miles of golden beaches have made tourism the most practical industry in these areas. Still, there is a danger that building too many hotels and resorts will harm the environment and beauty of these islands. The challenge to the people of the Pacific Islands is to maintain a balance, so that the tourist industry does not destroy what attracts tourists to these islands.

29

Discovery in the Depths

Guam is a vacationer's paradise. It offers warm, gentle weather, sparkling clear waters, and friendly people. It also has some of the most spectacular scenery in the world. For many visitors, Guam's best scenery isn't on the island itself. It's found in the water surrounding the island. That makes scuba diving big business in Guam. In fact, the island is home to the largest diving operation in the Western Pacific region. It is called the Micronesian Divers Association (MDA). It was founded in 1981. Since that time, the business has grown steadily. It's now a combination dive-training center, retail equipment store, and dive-boat charter service. The MDA also sponsors diving tours to other areas of the Pacific Islands such as the Northern Marianas.

The MDA has boats that take out tourist divers and local divers every day. It offers a choice of two different kinds of diving—inside Apra Harbor or outside it. The harbor is four miles long, a mile and a half wide, and, in some spots, 150 feet deep! It is protected from rough ocean winds, so the water is usually calm. Underneath that calm water lies a huge variety of diving attractions, including shipwrecks and sunken airplanes.

One of the most popular of these diving attractions is the *Tokai Maru*, a Japanese World War II cargo boat that was torpedoed and sunk in 1943. The boat is 465 feet long. It lies on its side and its mast reaches within 35 feet of the water's surface. On August 8, 1993, an earthquake that registered 8.2 on the Richter scale shook Guam. The vibration rocked the *Tokai Maru* and another nearby wreck, the World War I German cruiser SMS *Cormoran*, which was sunk in 1917. For years the two vessels had lain on the ocean floor within six feet of one another. But the movement of the earthquake created a strange picture. The *Tokai Maru* now lies on top of the *Cormoran*.

For beginning divers, a good wreck to explore is the American Tanker. This barge was used to move war materials during World War II. The tanker's deck is only fifty feet from the water's surface. Advanced divers enjoy exploring the *Kitsugawa Maru*, a Japanese World War II freighter. The

Truk Lagoon was the main anchoring spot for the Japanese Imperial Fleet during World War II. The Allied forces attacked Truk in February 1944, sinking sixty Japanese ships and aircraft. Since then, the lagoon has been a treasure chest for scuba divers.

Divers are exploring this twin engine bomber, which crashed during World War II. The bomber is lying on the ocean floor, fifty feet below the surface.

The view is spectacular in the ocean depths. On a clear day, divers can spot hundreds of different animal and plant species.

vessel still looks much the way it did before it was sunk. In fact, its guns are still mounted on its bow. Divers can check out the details at depths between 60 and 130 feet.

For divers whose interests lie outside war wrecks, the MDA offers dives that explore the coral reefs surrounding Guam. One of these reefs, Western Shoals, covers several acres. Although the top of the reef comes within ten feet of the ocean's surface, its sides drop off to depths of more than one hundred feet in some places. Another excellent diving spot is Hourglass Reef, where coral formations make up the underwater

landscape. At Hidden Reef, near the mouth of Apra Harbor, divers can see for distances of eighty feet because of the clear ocean currents.

Diving outside Apra Harbor provides many wonders, also. However, the waters beyond the harbor are not protected from wind and storms. Diving there requires a bit more skill—and good weather conditions. One of the most exciting dive sites outside the harbor is an undersea tunnel known as the Blue Hole. The tunnel's entrance is sixty feet below the ocean's surface. At the end of the tunnel—130 feet below the ocean's surface—is a steep drop-off. The water down there is very clear. Divers often report seeing schools of barracuda and whitetip sharks.

Some people enjoy diving at Shark Pit. It's a combination coral reef and underwater junkyard. The area was once used as a dumping ground for World War II military equipment. On the ocean floor lie trucks, jeeps, and other hardware—all of it covered with coral. South of Guam are sites that give divers the opportunity to explore fascinating varieties of Pacific Ocean life. Divers swim side by side with moray eels, angelfish, and lionfish.

Guam's reputation as a first-class spot for scuba diving is growing every year. More and more tourists are looking to add adventure to their relaxing vacations. Guam can supply plenty of excitement for these thrillseekers to take back home.

A diver enters a room of a sunken ship. Some of the shipwrecks in Truk Lagoon are as large as a fifty-story building.

Where Past and Future Meet

Guam and the Northern Marianas—like so many of the Pacific Islands—are a fascinating blend of East and West, modern and traditional. About 40 percent of Guamanians are Chamorros, descendants of the island's first inhabitants. Living side by side with these people are American military personnel, who make up one sixth of Guam's population. Guam has two official languages—Chamorro and English. Of the two, English is the most commonly spoken.

Of the United States territories in the Pacific Islands, Guam is by far the most prosperous. The island has a thriving tourist industry—and all the modern luxury hotels and conveniences to go along with it. In fact, many areas of Guam remind tourists of Honolulu, Hawaii. There are beaches, fine restaurants, and an exciting night life. There are also traffic jams and, as in most cultures, growing problems with pollution.

Within Guam's villages there is a more traditional way of life. Artisans weave baskets of intricate designs—some inset with shells. Other craftspeople

Both men and women in Micronesia have traditionally woven baskets and mats from plant fibers, such as palm tree fronds. This woman, who is from Saipan, is weaving a hat.

These people are attending church on Savaii Island in Western Samoa. Christianity is the main religion in Polynesia and has been since the late 1800s.

This mosaic depicts the story of two Chamorro lovers. Legend has it that they jumped off a cliff to their deaths when their parents refused to allow them to marry.

make elaborate woodcarvings, wall hangings, and hand-painted clothing.

Due to the early influence of Spanish missionaries, many inhabitants of the Pacific Islands practice Christianity. Each village has a yearly feast day devoted to its patron saint. The people of Guam and the Northern Marianas also enjoy many nonreligious gatherings. There are local fiestas throughout the year. At most of them, visitors are warmly welcomed.

In American Samoa, the traditional lifestyle and culture of the people is known as *fa'asamoa*, or "the Samoan way." Many Samoans live in fairly traditional villages where life is family centered. An extended family system works for the common good to preserve the island's natural resources. It has also been the key factor in maintaining the culture and folklore of the Samoan people. For three thousand years, Samoans have cared for their environment. In fact, the name the people gave their land reflects their attitude. *Samoa* means "sacred earth." Each extended family, or *'aiga*, chooses a chief, called a *matai*, who handles the family finances and settles family arguments. This person also represents the family in the village council, called the *fono*. The council makes final decisions about matters such as land use and fishing rights.

The language most often spoken in American Samoa is Samoan, which is a Polynesian dialect. Because of the extended American influence there, many Samoans also speak English.

As artisans, the Samoans are best known for their use of wood and fibers, their fine craftsmanship, and their unique designs. One example is the traditional *siapo* cloth made from the bark of the mulberry tree.

As American Samoa continues to modernize, much of its traditional way of life will probably change. Already many American Samoans have exchanged the fa'asamoa for the more American lifestyle of cities such as Pago Pago. They live in a modern world of fast food, automobiles, and other conveniences. They wear American-style clothes and shop for American food in supermarkets.

In American Samoa and throughout the Pacific Islands, young people are excited by the many foreign cultures they are exposed to in the media and in their own cities. But on all the islands people can still look out their windows and see evidence of traditional cultures many hundreds of years old.

Micronesians traditionally dance in either a standing or a sitting position. They make music with concussion sticks, which may be shaken or beaten together, or by singing.

The making of *siapo* cloth is a traditional Samoan craft. Samoans beat the bark of a mulberry tree into sheets, called *tapa*. They decorate the sheets and make them into clothing.

The Art of the Tale

The people of Guam have long been known for their imaginative folktales. These stories are passed down from generation to generation. Today's children listen to many of the same folktales their ancestors did. Some of these tell how or why well-known things came to be.

One such folktale tells of a great famine long ago in Guam. No crops grew on the land and the people were starving. Two brothers lived on opposite sides of the island. Each decided to search the other side of the island to see if the famine had reached that far. Each set off with his three children. When the two brothers met at the middle of the island, they realized that the famine was as bad as they expected. It had been days since any of them had eaten. Sad and tired they all laid down to sleep. In the morning the two brothers found that their children had died in the night. In great sorrow, they buried the children, putting stones at the heads of the graves. This act took all their strength and the brothers collapsed exhausted from

Breadfruit is a food staple in the Pacific Islands.

their labor. When they awoke they were astonished to find the gravestones were gone. In their place were trees covered with strange fruit. The brothers ate some of the fruit, which they called breadfruit, and stored some in their bags. They shared their food with everyone they met. From that day on, there was never another famine in Guam, thanks to the delicious and plentiful fruit known as breadfruit.

Another Guamanian folktale tells how a popular site got its name. There was a giant who lived on Guam long ago. He was the biggest, strongest man on the island, and he lived with his son on the beach at Apuguan. As time went by, the son also grew very large and strong. At first the father was proud of his child, but soon he began to fear that one day his son's strength would be greater than his own. One day when the son was only three years old, the son managed to pull up a young coconut tree by the roots. This show of strength so enraged the father that with a great bellow, he chased his son through the jungle. The terrified boy ran to the very tip of the north end of the island. His father crashed through the jungle behind him. With nowhere left to run, the young boy took a great running leap, which carried him across the water all the way over to the island of Rota. When he landed, his footprint sunk deep into the stone. Ever since, the spot where the boy landed has been called *Puntan Patgon*, or "Child's Point."

Folktales require a strong imagination and a sense of playfulness. These qualities have been lost in some cultures, but Guam upholds them. The children of Guam are brought up on a steady diet of imagination, wonder, and tradition.

In Polynesia, families customarily grow coconuts, breadfruit, and yams in their gardens. These men are preparing a breadfruit and coconut dish.

A National Park in the Pacific

The newest member of the United States National Parks family isn't in the continental United States. It's in the Pacific Ocean, about 2,300 miles southwest of Hawaii. The park covers a total of almost nine thousand acres, spread out over parts of three separate islands. It's a place of spectacular beauty, of sea cliffs, rain forests, and exotic flora and fauna.

The official name of this park is American Samoa National Park. However, that name is misleading because some traditional chiefs are reluctant to give up the property to the United States. Even though visitors are welcome within the park boundaries, the land area still belongs to the villages.

There are many Samoan cultural areas within the park, including archaeological sites and at least one prehistoric village. The islands of Ofu, Tutuila, and Ta'u each make up a part of the projected park area. These islands are home to an incredible variety of plant and animal life.

The largest part of the park—five thousand acres—is on Ta'u. Most of this area is untouched rain forest. On the island of Tutuila there is a nesting site for a variety of rare or endangered birds. To reach the park from the port city of Pago Pago, an aerial tram runs

The rain forests of American Samoa preserve a rich diversity of plant life, including many different kinds of ferns and orchids.

This beach is near Pago Pago, in the Tutuila Island section of the American Samoa National Park.

above the harbor, straight up to the top of Mount Alava. Off the tiny island of Ofu is thought to be one of the most perfect examples of a healthy coral reef in the Pacific.

American Samoa National Park was approved by the United States Congress in 1988. Samoan village chiefs have agreed to lease the land to the United States, but the two cultures have different ways of handling land agreements. For example, the American system is one of written records and contracts. The Samoan system is based on custom and oral agreement. A common way of finalizing the agreement has yet to be found.

In addition, not all village chiefs are in agreement about the need for a national park. "We've always looked after our forests," High Chief Gi M Malala of Pago Pago said. "Why do we need the Park Service?" Others believe the protection that a National Park Service would give is necessary to hold off destruction of the land through development. Talking Chief Tuaolo, one of American Samoa's highest-ranking leaders, is in favor of the park. "It will preserve our culture," he said.

American Samoa National Park is a test of the relationship between two diverse cultures. Both sides have much to gain by making sure everyone is satisfied with the agreement.

KODIAK
3325
PETROPAVLOSK 2645
BALI
MANILA 2775
HAROLD'S CLUB
4441
HONG KONG
TOKYO
2240
HONOLULU
2100
GUAM 1374

Education and Preservation

As the twenty-first century approaches, the pace of progress is speeding up all over the world. Nowhere is this more true than in the Pacific Islands. An expanded tourist industry is very much a part of the economic future of the islands. Great care and foresight will be needed to preserve the Pacific Islands' natural beauty and diverse cultures, while at the same time sharing these gifts with the rest of the world.

However, the people of the Pacific Islands realize that the success of these goals depend on their youth. The islands must offer young people enough opportunities at home to keep them from wanting to find these opportunities in the United States and elsewhere. That means making changes to their educational systems. Today, the goal in the Pacific Islands is to teach students management and leadership skills that will help develop new businesses.

There are already many high-quality private high schools on Guam, Saipan, and Chuuk. The University of Guam has one of the best oceanographic centers in

This signpost at Majuro International Airport in the Marshall Islands symbolizes the ongoing connection Pacific Islanders share with the rest of the world.

43

These children attend a school in Saipan. Pacific Islanders are adapting their schools to make education more effective for children who come from diverse cultural backgrounds.

the Pacific. The Northern Marianas and the Federated States of Micronesia are using schools to experiment with developing new educational programs. If these programs are successful, they will be expanded for use throughout the islands. Guam is working out new methods that involve parents, students, and the community in the education effort. In 1993 Guam's single highest expense—$209 million—was on education.

Pacific Islanders are becoming increasingly aware of the effects of progress on their traditional heritage. Organizations such as American Samoa's Council on Culture, Arts, and Humanities, for example, have been founded to increase public awareness and interest in the unique heritage of the islands. Each year such organizations publish books, produce exhibits, and sponsor classes on Pacific culture. The efforts of educational and cultural organizations will enable the Pacific Islanders to preserve their heritage while continuing to develop a self-sufficient economy.

Important Historical Events

1521 Ferdinand Magellan reaches Guam.

1565 Miguel López de Legazpi claims Guam and the surrounding islands for Spain.

1668 Spanish Jesuit missionaries arrive on Guam and the Marianas.

1680 to 1695 José de Quinoga wages war on the Chamorro population in an attempt to convert them to Catholicism.

1722 Dutch admiral Jacob Roggeveen explores the Samoan Islands.

1768 French navigator Louis-Antoine de Bougainville charts the Samoan Islands.

1839 American naval commander Charles Wilkes maps the Samoan Islands.

1867 The United States controls Eastern and Sand islands, the two islands that make up what is now Midway.

1879 Control of the harbor at Apia is disputed. Foreign warships anchor off the Samoan coast.

1889 The Berlin Treaty is signed.

1898 The United States seizes Guam. On August 12, the Treaty of Paris is signed, making Guam a U.S. possession.

1899 The Berlin Treaty is overturned. A new agreement gives Eastern Samoa to the United States and Western Samoa to Germany. Spain sells the Mariana Islands to Germany.

1904 Samoan chiefs sign over control of Eastern Samoa, which is renamed American Samoa.

1933 The Guamanian bill of rights is approved by the U.S. Congress.

1941 Japanese forces invade and occupy Wake Island and Guam.

1942 The United States Navy defeats Japanese ships in the Battle of Midway.

1944 American troops recapture Guam.

1945 The United States drops an atomic bomb on the Japanese city of Hiroshima.

1947 The United Nations group the Japanese-held Micronesian islands into a United States-run trust territory.

1950 President Truman signs the Organic Act.

1961 The United States launches a program to develop the economy of American Samoa.

1970 Guam elects its first governor.

1975 The Northern Marianas vote in favor of a political union with the United States.

1982 Guam votes to seek United States commonwealth status.

1986 The Northern Marianas become a commonwealth of the United States. An agreement with the United States divides the Caroline Islands into the Republic of Palau and the Federated States of Micronesia. The Republic of the Marshall Islands is established.

1990 The United Nations Security Council ends the trusteeship for all trust territories except Palau.

1992 Typhoon Omar devastates Guam.

1993 An earthquake rocks Guam.

1994 Palau becomes an independent nation.

Guam

Official Name. Territory of Guam

Capital. Agana

Bird. Toto (Fruit Dove)

Flower. Puti Tai Nobio (Bougainvillea)

Tree. Ifit (Intsiabijuga)

Nickname. Where America's Day Begins

Song. "Stand Ye Guamanians"

Languages. Chamorro, English

Status. Unincorporated, Organized Territory 1950

Government. Congress: One elected nonvoting in the U.S. House of Representatives. Territory Legislature: 21-person legislature whose members are elected every two years

Area. 209 sq mi (541 sq km)

Coastline. 78 mi (125.5 km)

Population. 1990: 132,726. Density: 590 per sq mi

Major Industries. U.S. military, tourism, petroleum refining

National Holiday. Guam Discovery Day, the first Monday in March

Seal

The territorial flag of Guam is dark blue with a red border. In the center is a red-bordered beach scene complete with outrigger canoe, a palm tree, and the word GUAM superimposed in red letters.

Northern Marianas

Official Name. Commonwealth of the Northern Mariana Islands

Abbreviation. CNMI

Capital. Saipan

Languages. Chamorro, Carolinian, English

Status. Commonwealth November 3, 1986

Government. Governor elected by popular vote. Nine-member Senate elected for four-year term; 15-member House of Representatives elected for two-year term

Area. 183.5 sq mi (477 sq km)

Coastline. 920 mi (1,482 km)

Population. 1994 Estimate: 56,656

Major Industries. Tourism, construction, light industry, handicrafts

National Holiday. Commonwealth Day, January 8

American Samoa

Official Name. Territory of American Samoa

Capital. Pago Pago, Island of Tutuila

Flower. Paogo (Ula-Fala)

Plant. Ava

Motto. *Samoa Muamua Le Atua* (In Samoa, God Is First)

Song. "Amerika Samoa"

Languages. Samoan, English

Status. Unincorporated, unorganized territory, Constitution ratified 1966, in effect 1967

Government. U.S. Congress: One nonvoting member. American Samoan Legislature: 18 senators chosen by county councils to serve four-year terms; 20 representatives elected by popular vote to serve two-year terms

Area. 77 sq mi (199 sq km)

Population. 1992 Census: 50,923

Major Industries. Tuna canneries, meat canning, handicrafts, dairy farming, tourism.

National Holiday. Territorial Flag Day, April 17

Index

3 0060 0002490 1